A Dartmoor Naturalist
Woodlands

Tony Hills

ORCHARD PUBLICATIONS
2 Orchard Close, Chudleigh, Newton Abbot, Devon TQ13 0LR
Telephone: (01626) 852714

ISBN 1 898964 43 2

Printed by:
Hedgerow Print, Crediton, Devon EX17 1ES

'The woods are lovely, dark and deep.
But I have promises to keep
And miles to go before I sleep.'

Robert Frost
*Stopping by Woods on a
Snowy Evening*

CONTENTS

PAGE

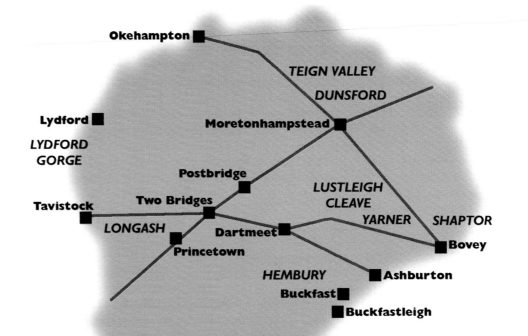

Okehampton

TEIGN VALLEY

DUNSFORD

Lydford

LYDFORD
GORGE

Moretonhampstead

Postbridge

LUSTLEIGH
CLEAVE

Two Bridges

YARNER   SHAPTOR

Tavistock

LONGASH   Dartmeet   Bovey

Princetown

HEMBURY

Buckfast   Ashburton

Buckfastleigh

Woodlands

Dartmoor – once spelt 'Dertmore' – probably never had many trees apart from birches, yet it was always called a forest: natural enough because 'forest' is from a Latin word foris, which means 'outside'. All the high, bare moorland was outside farmers' stone walls and fences and only rough tracks and muddy lanes linked the tiny hamlets and villages. Not surprisingly, many legends and traditions came to be linked with it but the moor's beauty and diversity are the chief reasons for its fame. Its upland heather is so important that the EC has included it as an area for special conservation measures in its Habitats and Species Directive; Dartmoor's boggy areas are also included, along with its caves and mines. These, together with Dartmoor's other archaeological and prehistoric sites, make it the most important area in the whole of Europe for such studies.

The woods themselves are as delightful as any to be found in Britain: if you want great displays of spring daffodils followed a little later by bluebells, or you want to see rare lichens, dormice or wood ants they can be found here. In fact some wildlife exists only on Dartmoor and is as a result highly endangered, so the more we can look after the valley bogs, the upland heathlands and the woods the better. Yet despite all our efforts some creatures and plants have become extinct in Britain even quite recently. An example is the butterfly known as the large blue: its very last site in 1979 was a grass field on the edge of Dartmoor. As for the skylark, which has vanished from much of Britain, it can still be heard over Dartmoor because these high heathlands are exactly what this bird likes best – so we may yet save it from extinction.

Spring is often the best time to visit the woods, because in this season the birds are at their busiest – and their noisiest with all the males declaring their territorial rights. On the other hand an autumn visit can be just as rewarding. Dartmoor's native trees are mainly the deciduous oaks which are at their best just before their leaves fall. Often they grow along river banks and a rocky tumbling stream overhung with oak and alder – a tree common on river banks or in wet woods – can be a marvellous sight. You will find these woods richly rewarding for rock forms, plantlife, birdlife or just for a day's outing. So take your pick – and your strongest boots.

LYDFORD GORGE

Lydford Gorge – Polypody fern on an ancient sycamore

How to get there
Grid Reference 509 843 (main car park)
From Okehampton take the A30 westwards and then the A 386 signposted to Tavistock. Take this A road for about five miles until you reach the Dartmoor Inn. Turn right here, signposted to Lydford, and carry on down right through the village to the National Trust headquarters for the gorge. The NT has the usual public amenities.

The one hundred and fifty acre gorge, which you could call ancient woodland as nobody has ever been silly enough to try to farm it, must surely be unique. Where else in Devon, or the rest of the United Kingdom for that matter, would you find a woodland walk with a waterfall at one end and a raging cauldron of water at the other. You could start walking from the waterfall end, where there is another car park, but it is perhaps best to begin at the main entrance, and simply follow the signs taking you along both sides of the gorge eventually, and ending at the Devil's Cauldron itself: a circuit of about three miles but you will see from a leaflet at the office that shorter walks are possible, and a part of the woodland at the waterfall end has a flat path for wheelchairs.

Lydford Gorge is one of the finest and best-known beauty spots in Devon: a densely-wooded ravine carved out by the Lyd river over millions of years. About four million years ago the Lyd 'captured' another one flowing in the opposite direction.

The force of water wears away the banks, and although in meandering rivers a piece of bank can by such means even become an island in time, the Lyd in this case met up with another and the two joined forces.

As you walk around you get the feeling of water dripping down from just about everywhere and in the process causing soil erosion. But plants slow up the erosion by means of their roots. The commonest plant here is woodrush with its deep-green, strap-like leaves, which people quite understandably mistake for bluebells – though there are plenty of these too. Where the exposed roots and dead woodrush leaves hang down incessantly dripping there is a distinct impression of equatorial jungle: a similar wet luxuriance but minus the heat. Moisture levels here are so high, even in sunny weather, that the gorge is a riot of ferns and mosses beneath the shade of the overhanging trees. The mosses are especially remarkable: even in towns you can sometimes see a little moss on tree trunks but here they smother them entirely, from ground level up into the branches as far as the eye can see. And so thickly that ferns such as the one called common polypody take root wherever boughs are made suitably wet by sponge-like moss. So sometimes it is hard to tell the tree species just by a glance at the trunk, because all you can see is moss. The entire gorge has such abundance of vegetation that it has been designated as a Site of Special Scientific Interest (SSSI).

It would be surprising if it had not been given this status as it contains the vast majority of woodland trees and plants – plus a sprinkling of conifers – which are genuinely native to the county. Their habitats vary according to levels in the gorge and it is easy to note the changes since the path ascends or descends for much of the route. Oaks dominate the gorge but there is plenty of hazel – once coppiced but no longer – plus fine specimens of beech, ash and sycamore, some of the latter being truly magnificent. There is even a leycesteria bush, which is anything but native as it comes from China. Perhaps it got here by a seed being washed out of someone's garden and then downstream into the gorge. Another non-native and doing nicely here is skunk cabbage, a North American plant with bright yellow spathes when flowering in early spring, its structure resembling the lords-and-ladies plant. It loves mud and rich soil and is conspicuous even out of season as it has huge plain leaves two feet or more in length. It is related to our arum lilies but its smell is quite off-putting. Wild garlic is also found in the gorge and a spring visit is to be recommended for the violets, primroses, wood anemones and the delicate-flowered wood sorrel with its trefoil leaf. The bluebells are at their best a little later, in May. There are some rare or very uncommon plants here too, such as the so-called luminous moss – not really luminous but it is a golden moss with a liking for dark crevices so it seems to shine in the gloom. And there are some rare liverworts encouraged by all the shady wetness. The gorge is rich in the fungus family too, like puffballs, earthballs, coral spot fungus and the prettily-named scarlet elf cup, bright scarlet inside the cup and growing on rotting logs or wet humus. Not a plant you will see except in western areas. In addition there is bracket fungus on some of the trees, which slowly kills them even if it takes years.

The White Lady Waterfall, named after some dubious legend, is much photographed and justifiably so. It streams down over the rocks in an unbroken drop of about one hundred feet into the Lyd below: where the two meet there is shallow, slow-moving water very attractive to dragonflies in particular. The largest, like the emperor dragonfly, are called hawkers because of the way they go up, down or around like a door-to-door salesman. Smaller ones are named darters and the smallest are known as damselflies – which can even fly backwards. Hawkers at rest always leave their wings open, but damselflies close them over their bodies much as butterflies do, so when resting it is easy to tell which is which by this difference in habit. Did you know they have teeth? Being carnivorous they use them for chewing up mosquitoes, for instance, so they are beneficial to us as well as beautiful. Sometimes there are salmon in this little river and always plenty of brown

Scarlet elf cup fungus, Lydford Gorge.

trout to see, a fish rarely over a foot long. The fish have a diet of molluscs, worms, and especially larvae like those of stoneflies. These spend much of their life crawling around on river-bed stones – which is perhaps the reason for their name.

There is plenty of gorge fauna apart from fish and insects. Birds include grey heron, kingfisher, grey wagtail and the wren-like dipper, which swims on or even walks under the river. All three woodpeckers, nuthatch and treecreeper are present, plus many more common in the west such as the buzzard. Higher and drier slopes have adders and even slow-worms, the legless lizard, in a few places. Badgers and grey squirrels are both busy here, the latter doing less harm to oaks than is often thought. Squirrels tend by preference to attack sycamore trees, which is a good thing because this species, superb as it can be when mature, is sometimes a nuisance like beech when its huge numbers of seeds germinate. Saplings of beech and sycamore get cleared by staff but the policy is to leave mature trees well alone unless there is good reason for felling: if an old tree is dying off then it may be cut down but not removed. On the ground it is a good wildlife food source.

The path heading back to the Devil's Cauldron gets narrower and more slippery. Dartmoor's granite is mostly in the central areas but here the rock is chiefly slate or shale, with a little limestone and quartz. So when wet it can be quite tricky to negotiate as the path is worn smooth in places. Occasionally you will find rails to hold on to but it is advisable to go carefully. In some parts the track is flat against vertical rock faces, so an eye-level inspection of dozens of different mosses and lichens is possible, with tiny inch-high hart's-tongue, for example, instead of the fully-grown ones a foot or more across. In places you almost feel you are rock-climbing, but there is little danger of stumbling down into the river if reasonable precautions are taken.

The mine shaft entrances occasionally to be seen are known as 'adits', some of which go only a few yards into the rock as no valuable minerals like tin ore are present. But others go a considerable distance and are now, having been disused ever since we started importing this metal, invaluable for bats to roost and hibernate in. This includes the highly endangered greater horseshoe bat of which few colonies remain. Chiefly as a result of human disturbance we have lost ninety per cent of them since the second world war. Bats also lose out when we convert old barns, or treat roof timbers with toxic chemicals to mention just two causes for their demise. At the Devil's Cauldron end of the gorge you may see odd-looking, wedge-shaped nest boxes on some of the trees; these are for bats, not birds, and especially for the tiny pipistrelle bat, which likes to use them for a summer roosting place.

In summer the larger boulders in the river look splendid: covered not just in bright green moss but with the pink flowers of purslane on them. It can be a stunning sight, these mini rock gardens with white water foaming all around them. And so also are some of the dead tree trunks lying across the stream,

LYDFORD GORGE

likewise a brilliant green.

As you approach Tunnel Falls the scenery becomes dramatic: moss and fern clinging to and hanging from every black and jagged-looking ledge of rock towering above you; as wild and romantic a spot as anywhere in the south-west. The further you go the narrower the ravine, with each side leaning towards the other. Some might just possibly feel it slightly claustrophobic with such massive rocks, with the other side only a few feet out of reach: black and forbidding but a jumble of vivid moss, rare liverworts, lichens and ferns make a striking contrast. Just before you reach the Cauldron itself the waters flow ferociously and deafeningly around hollowed rocks made glassy-smooth by millions of years of rushing torrents; this witches' brew seems dark and sinister even on a sunny day. But you may have to queue to see the Cauldron because the walkway to it only holds six people at any one time. No dogs or toddlers allowed on it – and there is a notice to this effect. Altogether a wonderful experience.

Mine adit, Lydford Gorge.

Oaks old and young – Hembury

How to get there

Grid Reference SX 729 686

From Exeter take the A38 in the Plymouth direction and stay on it until you reach the main Totnes-Dartington-Buckfastleigh junction. Here you take the bridge over the A38 in the Buckfastleigh direction. The road at once bears left to a small roundabout. Buckfast Abbey is signposted here to the right. Follow this sign, go past Buckfast Abbey entrance, then turn right signposted to Buckfast village. Go right through this village and turn right at a small crossroads. A few yards further on take a right turn signposted Hembury Wood. The main car park is on the left but if you want to park much higher up carry on a further mile or so to the car park on the right.

This is a very fine woodland – large compared with many – owned by the National Trust for over half a century and their policy is to manage it as a natural deciduous oak woodland, with hazel below the canopy of oak. Some deciduous trees such as Japanese larch were once planted here but they do not really belong in such a splendid native wood as Hembury and are being slowly removed. However there are also a few magnificent conifers like western hemlock which are being left much as the great beech trees are along the water's edge. You may notice a sprinkling of wild rhododendron, yew and fair amounts of holly. These add diversity but the rhododendron will be strictly controlled. The oaks are the sessile sort chiefly and there are considerable numbers of birch trees, both silver birch and downy birch, the latter being less elegant and graceful than the silver variety. Competition from other trees often makes the birch shoot up and become spindly. Because of this they

HEMBURY WOOD

River Dart at Hembury.

knotweed – always difficult to control as it is such an invasive species – and montbretia, which is usually an 'escapee' from somebody's garden. Hembury is so rich in flora it has been designated as an SSSI, containing as it does well over a hundred different species of plants and trees, all native to the area and not introduced.

As you leave the wetter riverside areas, having walked from the main car park, with their mosses and ferns – the royal fern grows luxuriantly in the boggier areas – you climb uphill and now pass bilberry, bramble and bracken – all like this better-drained but still damp soil. You may notice as you begin to go upwards a thin metal pipe protruding vertically from the ground for about ten feet. This is part of a pumping system which channels water from the stream into a tank, where it builds up enough pressure to pump the water, via a narrow, garden-hose type of piping back to the fields at the top of the wood to fill farmers' troughs for their animals. You may also see a ruined stone barn dating from the nineteenth century, originally intended for domestic animals, especially cattle. Other former activities at Hembury were charcoal-burning, of which there is still evidence, and copper mining: you can see a mine adit near the river, and this contains hibernating bats.

In spring and summer there are plenty of flowers: bluebells, daffodils and primroses, as well as tutsan (a hypericum like a mini Rose of Sharon) and golden rod, which is a close relative of the Canadian golden rod people often grow in their gardens. The yellow flowers include wood sage, wood spurge – a kind of euphorbia – and common cow-wheat. There are foxgloves, violets and many others.

tend to lack resistance to fungus attack, so quite a few can be seen rotting: but not necessarily on the ground, as the rot sets in long before they fall.

Other plants which are non-native here include Japanese

Coming out of the wood at the top you will notice a different scene. It is more park-like, with individual trees carefully left when the National Trust's contractors cut away all the bramble and much of the gorse. The bracken, valuable as it is, must nevertheless be cleared as it is far too invasive. So it is crushed by rollers several times a year and after four or five years of this treatment it gives up the struggle. Much of the gorse is left for wildlife shelter and colour – even in mid- winter – but it does get straggly when reaching its full height of eight or ten feet, which is not ideal for wildlife. The preferred policy is to encourage stands of it about seven years old. Ants – and there are plenty at Hembury – eat gorse seeds while the small birds found here, like the linnets, use well-established gorse scrub for both food and shelter. The linnets feed on both seeds and insects and there is no shortage of either at Hembury. Other birds commonly seen in this wood are the long-tailed tit and the woodcock: you are quite likely to 'flush' the latter as you go because it feeds on wet ground and rests on it during the day. It looks a bit like a partridge in size and flight but with a much longer beak for prodding soft soil when looking for food. Woodcock are present throughout the year but in spring and early summer many others fly in from abroad: wood warblers, willow warblers, pied and spotted flycatchers and redstarts ('start' means 'tail') to mention just a few. The jays and magpies of course are here all the time as they never seem to have any taste for foreign travel. Look for the green woodpecker higher up where the fields are: there are plenty of wood ants around the borders

Undisturbed birch log stack providing rich habitat – Hembury.

for it to feed on, as well as beetles and grubs of many other insects. In fields they will feed on grain as well. Insects include of course butterflies, especially the pearl-bordered fritillary which likes to lay its eggs on the dog violets commonly to be seen here.

HEMBURY WOOD

Of Hembury's mammals the most obvious are rabbits, in abundance despite the predators, which love this gorsy, heathery terrain where they have nibbled the grass down so much and just left acres of moss. A far rarer mammal is the dormouse, which the NT is doing its best to encourage by establishing nest-boxes for it a few feet off the ground wherever there is hazel and honeysuckle. They have had considerable success with this project. Mammals are mostly seen best at dusk, so a torch is useful if you go there late. Just as binoculars are in the summer if you want a good chance of spotting summer birds which are then often well hidden amongst the leaves. One of the attractions in winter, though, is the way the dark trunks of mature trees contrast with the light grey or silvery bark of their saplings tangled around them. Oak, for example, is surprisingly light in colour at this very early stage.

At the highest point above the river – and originally with great views all round – is Hembury 'castle', which now consists of the earthworks and defensive ditches, covering a couple of acres, of what was once an Iron Age hill-fort. The ditches can still be clearly seen despite being somewhat overgrown and with much soil having spread down into them. The exact age is not known but well over a thousand years after it was built a wooden castle of sorts was erected on top of it in medieval times. There is now no trace of this, but the area is still very attractive with its prominent hump dotted with one or two young oak trees and the soil beneath them being covered in vivid green moss. A notice-board on site gives further details. Don't miss it.

Hembury hill-fort.

Lush vegetation at Shaptor and Furzeleigh.

From the A382 roundabout at Bovey Tracey take the Moretonhampstead direction for about half a mile. Turn right at the sign pointing to a hospital and then, at the hospital itself, go up a narrow and quite steep lane until you come to the edge of the wood on the left. There is room for two or three cars to park here, and at one or two other places around the wood there are further parking spaces.

These woods are some of the most attractive within Dartmoor's boundary and a footpath goes through them. If you come straight from the depressing gloom of a mature conifer plantation to the oakwoods here the difference is almost startling. There is a sense of lightness and quiet singing enhanced by the far greater diversity of Shaptor with its ninety or so plant species recorded. And the birdlife is rich too: I saw hawks above the wood and disturbed owls inside it. With so many small birds and mammals – including rabbits around the perimeter – the birds of prey are not short of food, so it is tempting to call it Raptor Wood instead. Chaffinches and robins are common here but the spotted flycatcher is also conspicuous in summer, not because of appearance – in fact it is a rather dull grey with precious few spots – but because it never seems to vary its habit of sitting on a branch or fence-post, then darting out to catch an insect and at once returning to its perch. I have never seen it continuously hunt for flies as swallows or martins do.

The lightness of these woods stays even in the middle of

SHAPTOR AND FURZELEIGH WOODS

winter when all the leaves have gone. Oak is the dominant and natural tree here but there are numerous other species like sweet chestnut, beech, birch, ash, sycamore and many more, especially hazel. A few conifers and common laurel bushes grow here too. The Woodland Trust, which owns Shaptor and Furzeleigh, aims to keep it as a typical outer Dartmoor oakwood; so they are removing conifers and sycamore – the latter being a tree which seeds far too readily. It is a pity that oak is reluctant to spread itself as fast as sycamore, but some seasons there are very few acorns and even when there are plenty they stand not much chance of germinating. This is because an oakwood contains so many birds and mammals which love to eat acorns: think of the jays, the rooks and wood-pigeons which are present at Shaptor; or the squirrels and hordes of mice which eat them; wood-pigeons alone can each eat dozens of acorns every day in the autumn or winter. There are also species of wasps which inject oak leaves and twigs with an acid. This makes the oak create round galls – 'oak apples' – in which the wasp's larvae grow. It is a wonder that oakwoods ever manage to replace ancient ones which eventually after centuries die back and fall. Many of our native trees like oaks, which have been here ever since the last ice sheets left Britain at least ten thousand years ago, attract a host of plant, insect and bird species which exploit them as habitat and food source, sometimes severely. A couple of moth species, for instance, will strip oaks of their new spring leaves quite bare when they emerge as caterpillars.

The footpath to the Shaptor Rocks themselves is strenuous in parts but the route has such a variety of habitats – and unexpected things like disused mine shafts or striking rock formations: the latter you pass roughly halfway along the path, leaning at odd angles in the shade as if they are remnants of ancient settlements – or a giant's mausoleum if you care to imagine them as such. But really they are just huge boulders half submerged in vegetation. You tend here to forget you are slowly getting higher even though the path may occasionally slope down rather than up and thus give the walker a bit of a breather. It hardly seems like a part of Dartmoor, but then the route crosses here and there what the botanists call a 'flush', which is typical of the moor. A wet flush is an area of extremely soggy soil – almost a bog but not quite – supplied by ground-water in a badly-drained patch often caused by the underlying rock. These occur in shady parts of Shaptor where several fern species are evident, like hart's-tongue and the royal fern or the very common one known as broad buckler fern, which can grow almost as big as the royal fern. Hart's-tongue can grow in very deep shade and can be found sometimes a few feet down a mine shaft entrance. There are of course plenty of mosses and liverworts as well as ferns – the liverworts having been given that name because they resemble a green version of the lobes of a liver, or a green seaweed. They are often found in wet places with mosses. In damp but less boggy sections look out for enchanter's nightshade, though when you have found it you may well ask yourself why you bothered – for this magic-sounding name it is certainly a pretty insignificant-looking flower. What makes it have such a name? This plant, a close relative of the much brighter rosebay willowherb and the evening primrose, was once used for a supposed medical benefit in its root and folklore suggests it was therefore applied by witches and other sorcerers. It is certainly odd in being almost the only common plant – and it is common enough in shady places in Devon and many other counties – to have just two petals per flower: in fact everything about it seems to be in twos, with its leaves in pairs, two stamens in each flower and then later on a pair of seeds in each pod. A weed not easy to get rid of if it pops up in the garden but its tiny pale pink or whitish flowers and heart-shaped leaves make it not entirely unattractive.

As you get higher up the path such flowers disappear quite suddenly and the numerous oaks and hazels look more stunted by the drier conditions; so there is more gorse, heather and rough grass, along with bracken of course. When you arrive at the Shaptor Rocks themselves you will see a memorial stone dedicated to a founder-member of several conservation bodies such as the Devon Wildlife Trust – but no sign of the rocks. They are concealed by scrub and bracken a short distance behind the memorial plaque, but it is worth pushing your way through the undergrowth because of the splendid views southward over both the Bovey and Teign estuaries and north overlooking the Wray Valley. The rocks themselves have been eroded to smooth protrusions partly covered in heather and fescue-type grasses able to stand the very dry conditions they often have to put up with because there is little soil to stop the rain running away or evaporating rapidly. Where the rocks are completely bare the mosses and lichens are about the only plants

Heather on the hill-top – Shaptor and Furzeleigh.

that can cling on. Still, you feel you deserve a rest here – and you can be certain while you enjoy the great panorama all around that the return trip is going to be a lot easier.

DUNSFORD WOOD

Path beside the River Teign – Dunsford.

How to get there
Grid Reference SX 805 884 (Steps Bridge)
From Exeter on the B3212 the distance is about nine miles. Arriving at Steps Bridge you will see on the right by the side of the bridge the reserve entrance. If coming from Moretonhampstead on the same road the distance is shorter, just over three miles, with the entrance now on your left at the far end of the bridge. Parking facilities are just a few yards away and Steps Bridge Hotel is also close to the river.

The National Trust own the wood, which is one of Devon's great beauty spots. It is actually managed by the Devon Wildlife Trust, which publishes leaflets and booklets about it and these are available on site. The wood's chief attraction for most people is the vast masses of wild daffodils growing along the valley floor. These are at their best in March and early April and they flower here along the banks of the Teign in perhaps greater profusion than anywhere else in the south-west. They love damp conditions and a rich soil: both are provided by the Teign overflowing as it often does. When that happens the river waters drop their mud on the valley floor because, once out of the river, the water no longer flows so mud particles just sink. This makes a 'nutrient-rich' soil with minerals washed down from Dartmoor. This feeds the daffodils and the bluebells and white wood anemones, both of which flower a little later. People unfortunately tend to tread on the leaves of these in their anxiety not to crush any daffodils as they photograph them. Bluebell leaves resemble grass somewhat so naturally they get stepped on, with damage to the invisible buds. Both Trusts stress how important it is and how beneficial for the flowers if all visitors keep to the paths. It does help conservation enormously.

The valley slopes are boulder-strewn, with a very thin soil quite different from that under the daffodils. So gorse, heather and bracken cling on here with their fibrous roots, with the gorse often making a fine background with its golden-yellow flowers visible through the trees, which at daffodil time are mostly still leafless as it is a deciduous wood. Some of the birches are enormous – I have never seen bigger or taller ones anywhere. If there are acorns on the oaks they will look rather small and rough and they will seem to sit on the branches rather than at the end of a stalk. This is a feature of the commonest species of oak tree on and around Dartmoor botanists call 'sessile'. Oaks with stalked acorns are 'pedunculate' oaks. Sessile means sitting. Most oaks in England in non-western areas are the pedunculate type, but the sessile oak seems tougher and generally smaller than the species with stalked acorns. Sessile oaks grow high on the moors, where they may have to tolerate harsh weather and little soil. Apart from the daffodils – which incidentally are the genuine native wild ones and therefore smaller than garden daffs and perhaps more attractive – there are several other very noticeable ones such as the wild garlic or ramsons, always a pleasure to see in the spring with its masses of white flowers. Another moisture lover here is pink purslane.

Dunsford also has a few rare mosses on the rocky areas up the valley sides. Even rarer here in similar habitat to the mosses is a hypericum – found in only three places in Devon. Rose of Sharon is a well-known relative, also yellow of course, but the flowers of this garden plant are very much bigger.

The river and damp meadows appeal to dragonflies and several butterflies, including the fritillaries with their richly chequered wings of light brown dotted with darker brown spots looking almost black. Some of these are now so scarce nationally that drastic action is being taken to prevent them becoming extinct. A fairly common butterfly, not endangered as yet, is the brimstone: a large, rich-yellow insect which is very noticeable though not just for its colour. It hibernates but tends to emerge even in winter on warmish days or in early spring when it stands out if it is the only one. 'Brimstone' is an old word for sulphur so the name is apt.

Birdlife at Dunsford is very varied largely because the woodland is itself diverse. Nearly all the trees are deciduous and the past management policy of coppicing some but not all trees means that their different ages and states of decay, if any, offer a wide range of habitats. This also applies to Yarner and both are very good bird-watching sites. In midsummer both these reserves tend to be a lot quieter when the birds are feeding their young than in the spring when nest-building is the chief activity. Notice the nest-boxes, which have greatly helped to attract more pied flycatchers. These birds seem to find such nest-boxes irresistible. In fact at Yarner Wood they never had pied flycatchers until nest-boxes were put up – after which they had plenty. So where did they all suddenly come from? The flycatchers are summer migrants here so a visit after the daffodils have gone offers the best chance of seeing them. They

DUNSFORD WOOD

feed on hosts of insects attracted to riverside plants such as the introduced Himalayan balsam.

With plenty of small animals in the wood and surrounding fields, along with many of the commoner birds, means that hawks are around. Of these the buzzard is the most easily recognised – or is it the kestrel? The buzzard is larger and never hovers like the kestrel but sails and drifts in circles on its great wings like a rudderless boat. The sparrow-hawk – also present – differs in its methods from the others by seldom going more than a few yards above the ground: it just flits along the quiet side of a hedge, then over it in a flash to pounce on unsuspecting birds which are by no means always sparrows. It kills anything up to the size of a wood-pigeon. Most of these small birds and their predators tend to associate with hedges and open fields as much as woodland. The same goes for magpies but never for jays; these chatty and bright birds, which not surprisingly are known to ornithologists as Garrulus, keep to the woods like treecreepers and nuthatches, but these two at times work their way along hedges with a few trees. Nuthatches, like greater spotted woodpeckers, will jab away at peanuts hung up originally to entice other birds while the mouse-like little treecreeper will search for insects on posts or chicken-run poles at times. Dunsford is a good place to watch them on big trees.

A visit in late autumn is suitable for a fungus foray: the famous stinkhorn, for example, known to botanists as Phallus impudicus. With a shape like that what else could it be called? You may also find some of the Amanita group in this reserve, including the one called false death cap.

A rare insect here is the wood cricket; a kind of grasshopper active by day in the leaf litter along the sunny edges of the trees. Easily missed, it being a drab grey, but with any luck you may hear it 'singing' like other grasshopper species. August and September is the best time for this. The Devon Wildlife Trust says they occur mainly in the New Forest but they live here too and at other Devon sites like Woodbury Down. They prefer warm spots as much as the house cricket does, which is often found near ovens indoors. If wood crickets are happy in their habitat they may keep chirping for hours whereas the grasshopper goes quiet for minutes at a time between songs.

Notices at Dunsford ask visitors to stay away from the water's edge because of soil erosion, caused not only by flooding but by too many people. Look at all the exposed alder roots and you will see how bad it is. The roots normally resist erosion of the banks but here they seem to be losing the battle. So this is another good reason for keeping to the paths.

Lichens on old birch – Yarner.

How to get there
Grid Reference SX 778 787
From the Bovey Tracey roundabout on the A382 take the B3387 towards Widecombe. After a mile or so you will see on the right a turning signposted Manaton. Follow this road for a further mile until you come to Yarner.

This National Nature Reserve offers the visitor a three-mile walk, partly along the valley but also up and down the slopes – with short cuts for those feeling lazy. It is a centuries-old wood which in 1952, when the authorities decided to give it NNR status and thus more protection, was not thought of as any special place as there were then so many similar oakwoods on Dartmoor fringes. But today it is highly valued, not least because so many of England's deciduous oak copses and woods were cut down during the second world war and for decades after that war ended.

Oak is the most important of all our trees for wildlife so Yarner's management policy is to keep it as such. But when it was bought for conservation nearly half a century ago it was felt that the wood needed a greater mix of tree species, so beech and a few conifers were planted. But beech, sycamore and rhododendron are a real threat, beautiful as they are, because beech shades out nearly everything when fully grown – even oak. So most of these trees have been cut down. The result is much greater light levels reaching the ground, which naturally benefits our native shrubs and trees and thus the insects, the birds and mammals find a better habitat. The right amount of light is extremely important where ferns, mosses and lichens are concerned because some of these just refuse to grow without the correct shade and moisture.

Yarner is now very attractive with its wooded, steeply-sloping valley sides, which were once partly open grazing fields, and it includes patches of real Dartmoor with heather and gorse. The oaks used to be heavily coppiced here to provide charcoal for smelting copper ore which came from a mine in this wood. In coppiced woods the trees are cut down close to the ground, but the stumps are left to grow again. Young oaks have a lot of tannin in their bark, and this was very useful in the leather industry. Remnants of such activities can be clearly seen as you walk, and notice the empty channel in the woods. This was dug mid-nineteenth century to supply water from Becky Falls to the Bovey Potteries then existing. Note the granite rails: L-shaped so that trucks carrying granite blocks from Haytor Quarry to Teigngrace were not derailed.

Yarner has acres of birch trees and their tiny seeds are very useful autumn and winter food for the birds. Chaffinches are keen on them but so are other finches such as the siskins – in winter the birches and alders make up a good deal of their diet. Birch is very tough and aggressive, competing with heather on poor soils, to the detriment of the common heather in time. So Yarner's policy is to burn such areas periodically: it is now the turn of the heather to look tough as it normally survives such treatment which kills the birch. But the latter has a trick up its sleeve as it can germinate its seeds in these blackened areas very quickly, precisely because it needs bare soil for this

purpose. A lightly-burnt area will soon show tiny birch trees, but as they only live about as long as the average human being does you will see at Yarner many dead ones, often covered in ivy. Trees are never strangled by ivy as people sometimes think: it simply uses the trees for support and in doing so it is very valuable indeed for wildlife. If you grow it up your house you will find it keeps the walls bone dry, so never cut it down. For shelter, for its flowers and berries it should always be preserved.

Rotting birches also attract fungi: one is a saucer-shaped bracket fungus called razor-strop, which grows on the trunk. Its tiny threadlike roots penetrate the wood much as dry rot fungus does, slowly killing the tree as it goes. Another fungus, under birches but not actually on them when still standing, is the fly agaric with its vivid scarlet cap and warty white spots. Holly is not quite as valuable for wildlife as ivy is but useful for its berries and also for the tiny leaf miner. This is a caterpillar so small it is actually inside the leaf – its larder – which it eats, leaving squiggly channels as it goes. Why are holly leaves often prickly lower down but not higher up? Perhaps evolution has trained it to produce spines where the danger of being eaten by animals is greatest.

Watch out for honeysuckle at Yarner and if you find any of its bark peeled off that would suggest dormice are present. They use it for nests. Unlike other small mammals – and dormice are a mere three inches long not counting the tail – they hibernate. 'Dormouse' means 'sleeping mouse' and sleep it does, in its cosy dormitory, for months. It curls up hedgehog-fashion, its bushy tail around it like a duvet – yet it goes very cold. It has to. Its body temperature goes so low it almost seems dead. But there is purpose here: no energy is needed where normal body processes like metabolism shut down – and no energy demands mean no food is required.

At Yarner you are bound to see ants' nests as there are hundreds of them, often in a sunny spot near birches. Listen carefully and you can hear them at work with bits of dead leaf, seeds or caterpillars being taken underground, where there may also be beetles. These supply the ants with a sugar solution, the ants in return giving them some of their own grubs to eat.

Bracken – that Dartmoor plague – is the commonest fern here, attractively uncurling its fronds in spring or changing to rich autumn colours later. In the wood's wettest spots look for what botanists call Osmunda regalis – the royal fern. One of our most beautiful, a deep-rooted clump growing a yard high, with fronds all around it gracefully drooping and several feet in length. A truly outstanding plant – no wonder they called it regalis.

Yarner foxes love eating fungus, bilberries and blackberries if voles and rabbits are in short supply for any reason. Badgers add acorns to their diet and, surprisingly, will eat wasp caterpillars if they can reach a nest, just as the green woodpecker with its long sticky tongue does. All three of our native woodpeckers are present here, as are lizards. In fact Yarner is quite remarkable for its wealth of animal life – its fauna including at least twenty different mammals, the majority of which will be found around the woodland edges; and it is so rich in moths and butterflies, over six hundred species recorded,

that this nature reserve is reckoned to be one of the very best in the United Kingdom. Two leaflets, a nature trail one and a woodland walk guide are available. Routes are waymarked with numbered posts and the leaflets tell you what to look for. The staff feed the birds from October to March so a winter visit to the observation hide is rewarding.

Up on Yarner's heather and gorse area watch out for that rarity, the Dartford warbler, which unlike many warblers braves our winters. In summer there are even nightjars here – but you will be very lucky to see one: they lie on the ground during the day but are brilliantly camouflaged.

Yarner Wood is educational as well as delightful, and its work is highly valuable. It shows you how seeming to do nothing at all is often better than interfering. Their motto could well be 'let sleeping logs lie' – if the logs are rotting down to serve as food and shelter for other wildlife higher up the food chain. In nature you can truthfully say that nothing at all is ever wasted.

LONGASH WOOD

Wet woodland – Longash.

How to get there
Grid Reference SX 553750
From Moretonhampstead take the B 3212 across the moor in the Princetown direction. From here follow the road signposted Tavistock. Merrivale quarry will clearly be seen ahead of you just off the right-hand side of the road. On the left there is space for parking just before crossing Merrivale Bridge and a few yards further down you will see a wooden signpost indicating a bridleway to the left. Take this path through two farmyards and you then arrive at the wood.

The oaks and hazels – the latter coppiced a long time ago – are only a few minutes away from where you left the car. If there were a competition to choose Dartmoor's most beautiful and haunting wood then Longash might well win it. Just after leaving the second farmyard the path takes the walker over a loudly gushing tributary of the Walkham river down on your right. Incidentally there is no circular walk here as the banks of the river are impassable. You could of course veer off to your left – though the notices advise you rightly enough to keep to the path – and return to the parking space by crossing the moor; but it is rough going. After a mile or so you will probably want to go back the way you came in any case, because these marvellous woods are well worth a second look. It is incredible what a combination of rock, water, moss and tree can create if totally left alone as they are here. Some of the path has dry-stone walling of granite blocks, now very old and covered with moss an inch or two thick in some places and as there are hundreds of foxgloves in the nooks and crannies left this path must be lovely in later spring and early summer when they are in flower.

A few yards further on from the tributary just mentioned you see the wood at its best: water cascading down from the Hucken Tor area and over a crazy paving of brilliant green humps, which of course turn out to be variously-sized boulders deep in moss, lichen and fern with a tangled canopy of hazel and oak above them. The usual wood sorrel, bramble and bracken are present, with hawthorn, blackthorn (sloe) common gorse, birch and rowan around the edges, which is where you will also find wood-rush and bluebell. The damp stone walls – the woodland is an SSSI and is partly a system of small, neglected fields with stone boundaries – are an excellent habitat for common navelwort and English stonewort amongst the mosses: as at Lydford Gorge the tree trunks are smothered and you can even find the navelwort growing in clumps on them where the ivy allows the space. Further along boulders dominate the scene although the oaks here are just as frequent. The boulders have had millions of years of erosion so in some places they lie there smooth and rounded, as if gently placed in layers on top of each other: not that there was anything gentle about their initial settlement when the extruded granite pushed up from deep down, a mass of white-hot molten rock. No shortage of moss, hard fern and spleenwort here as well as bilberry or whortleberry.

It is worth going on through the wooden gate, not only because of more woodland but also because the terrain opens out to a drier area of gorse and heather, plus a great view over the valley. Eventually this habitat gives way slowly to green fields – but notice on the way back the woodland fields, which are extremely soggy despite sloping down fairly steeply to the river. A lot of vegetation such as bracken and oak suddenly gives up at this point, with soft rush, sedges, species of sphagnum moss, grasses and marsh thistle taking over – the latter stands out because it is so tall. About the only tree able to cope with all the wet is the goat willow, which increases along with alder trees down by the river. Here there are also some ash trees which presumably gave the wood its name. Two sorts of violet grow at Longash – but not the sweet violet. One is the wet-loving marsh violet and the other is the common dog-violet, which has pinker petals and less heart-shaped leaves than its marsh relative. A species of forget-me-not and devil's-bit-scabious are also to be found at Longash – the scabious in particular has a liking for rough, damp and grassy places. Another plant to be found here associated with dampish hedges is the greater stitchwort, which is much more attractive than its common cousin, chickweed. It is a weak-looking spring-flowering plant with delicate leaves and each of its white petals curiously split down the middle – which is partly what gives it appeal.

The sphagnum mosses at Longash are the most important plant on Dartmoor, since the bogs consist of little else. Without them and their ability to hold on to water as efficiently as any sponges, a lot of Dartmoor would not exist. In the past they have been immensely useful much as bracken was; sphagnum began forming what is known as 'blanket' bog on Dartmoor at least five thousand years ago and has ever since been used, dried, as poultry or stable litter, as plant compost or cut-flower packing and even as bandages in wartime when these were in short supply. In Widecombe in the Moor on one of the National Trust properties there is a plaque in memory of those who collected and dried the sphagnum for this purpose during the first world war. It was as antiseptic as bandages because of an acid in it called sphagnol; and highly efficient in stopping the flow of blood by being so absorbent. These mosses are also very attractive to look at, especially in the autumn, ranging as they do from palest green to vivid emerald, subtle crimsons, wine reds and browns. Their colours vary from species to species as there are several sorts of sphagnum moss. As for lichens, perhaps the most interesting in this wood is the string-of-sausages one, which botanists have put in the Usnea family of bearded lichens. Like many of these it hangs down, greyish-green, from branches but the older stems become swollen into segments resembling strings of sausages making garlands all over the branches. Many lichens – and this is one of them – simply will not grow unless the air is very clean. So in most of England it is absent apart from western areas. But Dartmoor could be threatened if global warming means drastic climate changes: certainly the sphagnum would not survive any permanent, severe rainfall reduction – which would also be followed by wildlife disaster. One scientific report in 1996 said that if the bogs did dry up the insect life would disappear too. The report was not exaggerating, because insects play an indispensable part in nature; how would the swallows and bats – to mention only two out of hundreds of creatures – cope without them?

There are endless food supplies at Longash for squirrels, mice, badgers and other insect eaters. Ignore the obvious insects around, like the flies and bees: just brush aside a little leaf litter from around one of the boulders, for example, and you are sure to disturb centipedes, woodlice, beetles and numerous smaller organisms like springtails. These tiny creatures, which by means of their tails spring up when disturbed, are close relatives of the silverfish people sometimes find in their kitchens; or in their books as well, because they have a taste for eating glue – or at least sniffing it.

String of sausages lichen, Longash Wood.

Donkey's Cave – Lustleigh Cleave.

How to get there
Grid Reference SX 766 818 (Raven's Tor)
From the village of Lustleigh, by the church, take the road signposted Rudge ½. Turn right at Rudge Cross signposted Cleave. Go ¾ of a mile and park close by some metal railings bordering a field with ancient oaks. Walk two minutes in the same direction, past some houses and a bridleway entrance. The start of the walk is just a few yards further, on the left.

The walk, which is another Devon beauty spot, leads across a small field and then steeply upwards into a very remarkable wood, a tangle of huge trees and gigantic boulders.

Some of these rocks are deeply moss-covered yet softly folded together as if someone had done it carefully to create almost cavernous glooms which here and there are pitch-black; one such is Donkey's Cave – given the name because working donkeys used it for shelter. These are not really caves but the granite boulders have that effect. Some have trees appearing to stand sentinel outside or even springing from the boulders, in such a way you could easily mistake the trunks for the rocks. In many places tiny circular spots of bright green stand out against very dark moss: these are the young leaves of navel-wort, a very common plant in Devon: each leaf has a depression in the middle and it certainly resembles a navel – so much so the botanists decided to call it Umbilicus. It likes acid stone walls just as other members of the stonecrop family do and many rocks are smothered in it.

Although the woodland is mainly oak-hazel in nature with a great deal of bramble and bracken below, there are fine specimens of other trees; in particular the common holly, which here grows truly enormous. Notice also the long-neglected stone boundary walls – with so much moss it is hard to know they are in fact man-made structures. Flowering plants are few in number here because the shade and acid soil do not encourage them; even the blackberries fruit poorly for lack of light but the fungi, ferns and ivy do well. There is the conspicuous hart's tongue fern – our only one with solid, undivided leaves – in the shade and damp but there is also moonwort, a quite rare fern today, growing in the higher and grassier spots.

The wood opens out at the top, but there are still plenty of jumbled boulders. Here the extra light increases the diversity of plants so that they can grow deep down in the rock crevices hidden away from wind. From the top of the ridge there are excellent views across the valley and you can now begin to hear the river way down below. The Cleave is really like a huge, horizontal spine dotted with innumerable rocks on either side. The path slowly leaves behind the woodland proper and scrub, some of it blackthorn and broom, briefly replaces it. A little further on the gorse takes over, a surprisingly beautiful sight even as late as October. 'Cleave' is probably a different spelling for 'cliff' and certainly you get an impression of standing on top of a cliff here. There are wood ants in scattered colonies and the Cleave used to be a habitat for a species of ant now very rare – the narrow-headed ant, which no longer exists on Dartmoor. It disappeared from here about ten years ago but is still in Devon – and Scotland. No other English county has it, so it is a subject for protective measures. Other invertebrates include spiders and beetles, the latter attracted to

Dartmoor pony dung and unless you pick your way carefully it is easy to tread on these insects as they follow the paths taken by the ponies. There are also scarce butterflies here as well as common sorts: the purple emperor and brown hairstreak are both uncommon enough to be of some conservation concern.

The route takes you slowly down to Foxworthy Bridge: as bridges go it is small and unimpressive but the boulder-cluttered stream it spans is beautiful at this point. The walk now turns so that you go back towards the start – but a lot lower down. You may begin to feel all the best part is high up where you were a few minutes ago. But do not be disappointed: further splendid woodland has still to be gone through. Here the woods have little of the heaviness seen on the first part of the walk: the sense of lightness is largely due to the difference in tree species: there are of course oaks, but now the birches dominate the scene for a bit and as they have not been coppiced there are some huge specimens as big as those at Dunsford. Large boulders draped in moss seem more sunk in the leaf litter – another reason for the open feel.

As for the fauna there is no shortage. Birds include the ever-vocal robin and members of the tit family: not just the common blue and great tit but also the long-tailed tit: I disturbed a party of them up in the scrubby area and heard their typical tsi-tsi-tsi calls before I actually saw them. Stonechats like the Cleave too, because of all the gorse for its insects and as a place to nest: there must also be plenty of mice around to judge from all the buzzards, and certainly there are dormice. The proximity of farmed fields means that magpies are present, and likewise the jays in the woods. Both species like a varied diet, which unfortunately includes the eggs of smaller birds and often their nestlings. Other birds to be seen here may be the heron, pied flycatcher, redstart and wood warbler. These last three are summer visitors, but a winter resident is the lesser spotted woodpecker, a small and shy bird less spotted than most. In a way it is like our purple emperor butterfly in tending to stay high up in big trees and so well out of sight. But the butterfly does sometimes descend to the ground to suck liquid dung or mud when it needs a change from the honeydew on the oak leaves. So with luck you may see it.

Like many other woodland edges with gorse and heathery terrain Lustleigh Cleave is rich in spiders – huge numbers in fact in these drier areas especially, because the vast majority keep well away from water. They hardly need pure water in any case as they are all carnivorous and get their liquid from blood. The wolf spiders are very noticeable: called 'wolf' not because they hunt in packs but because they chase and run down their prey instead of waiting to ambush the various grasshoppers, woodlice and so on, which is what our familiar garden spider – also called diadem spider – does by building its beautiful orb nest across the bushes. A highly-skilled labour but spiders have been doing this for at least three hundred million years so they are good at it.

The wolf spiders either weave none at all or they construct, often at or near the bottom of gorse, heather and bracken, those conspicuous sheets of silk with a hole in the middle: something like a silvery funnel or whirlpool, which may lead down below ground level. These webs look much more attractive than those limp and shapeless webs you can see on old garden walls, for example – these are made by a different species. The wolf spider

From the top of the Cleave.

webs are often triangular in shape and a bit like the ones made indoors by house spiders. As for the food they eat this is often made up of springtails found so much in leaf litter and soil. Anything bigger, such as a beetle, can quickly be turned into an edible crumble, just before being eaten, by the spider injecting digestive juices.

If you are interested in archaeology the Cleave has plenty to investigate: some of it prehistoric such as the stone-built hill-fort which probably dates back to the Iron Age. There are also medieval field-banks and even the remains of a ridge-and-furrow system of ploughing. This is also likely to be medieval in origin and may have been practised to improve soil drainage.

Ancient beech trees – Charles and Hannicombe.

How to get there

Grid Reference 743 899 (Fingle Bridge)

From Whiddon Down take the A382 towards Moretonhampstead. At Sandy Park take the left turn signposted Drewsteignton and Fingle Bridge. Follow the Drewsteignton signs to Fingle Bridge down a steeply wooded road as far as the river. Park here on the left, just before the pub, or go over the bridge and park on the left.

The woodlands stretch both downstream to Clifford Bridge and upstream to Castle Drogo. Much woodland in the Teign Valley is privately owned or privately managed in agreement with the Dartmoor National Park Authority. Walks are available to the public as a result of negotiations between the bodies concerned and printed leaflets of some of the walks are obtainable.

Charles and Hannicombe Woods.

There is lovely scenery at Fingle Bridge and a few yards from it you enter these woods. Here you will see a signpost, with one of its arms pointing to Cranbrook Castle, well above the river. It is a fairly steep walk through the trees to the 'castle' – which is really an Iron Age fort – but the path zigzags along to the top and is therefore easier than it would otherwise be. As you go through this deciduous woodland you pass plenty of bracken, gorse, bilberry, a few patches of heather, wood ants galore and, at one point, a truly beautiful view across to Castle Drogo.

The fort itself is easily missed: where the path flattens out at the top look for a gate on the right. Go through it and then through lots of waist-high bracken till you come to the remnants of what was once a settlement, now half-hidden in heather, grass and bramble. Magnificent views all round and so high here the oaks, the few mountain ash and hawthorns are doomed never to grow up but remain stunted, with abundant moss and lichens on them; even the foxgloves look deprived and lost. The lack of soil and wind-swept nature of the place naturally favour the shorter plants like the tiny blue milkwort you come across or, more conspicuous, the bright yellow but small potentilla – tormentil. A rich-yellow plant very common along Devon's woodland edges or on the grassy moors and once used as a painkiller to alleviate torments if the name is an accurate indicator.

It is still possible to follow the circular construction of the fort with its stone walls and ditches now half full of turf and gorse, etc. It is so high you actually look down, not up, at Castle Drogo, yet despite its bleak nature even a few butterflies visit the area if they have a strong enough flight. It can be quite warm out of the wind in one of the overgrown ditches, which is where I found to my surprise a clouded yellow, a butterfly normally to be seen along the southern Devon coastal areas in summer. In winter it stays further south in Europe or parts of northern Africa. A really beautiful butterfly, not unlike a smaller version of the brimstone. Both prefer open spaces as does the painted lady, but woodland paths attract several others: an oakwood path is a likely habitat for the purple hairstreak, very much a lover of oak leaves for its grubs to eat, but sometimes it does fly lower down if there is honeydew around.

So high here the trees give up.

Fingle Woods have many fern species – though Britain has only a few of the thousands of species that exist globally – and an interesting one is the hard fern, dark or light green depending on shade and situation. A distinct fern because, although it has the usual fronds spreading out evenly around, it also sends up from its centre one or two more vertical fronds which look and feel hard and wiry with their very much narrower leaflets. These are the fertile fronds – all the other drooping ones are sterile – and on their undersides they carry the spores which are the first stage of the reproduction process.

The edges of these woods have fine specimens of oak, ash and beech, the latter often planted either for its sheer beauty or

TEIGN VALLEY WOODLANDS

Bilberry, bracken, birch and oak –
Charles and Hannicombe.

the smooth, dense quality of its timber. (The beech nuts of trees much further east, like those of the Chilterns, used to be called 'buck' – which gave Buckinghamshire its name). Sometimes hedge beeches were cut down, with the base left to grow on again. In time several trunks arising from the same bole would compete with each other and in doing so produce some attractive shapes, however distorted. Beech does in some years and especially after a warm summer offer a rich harvest of its nuts (beechmast) and this is invaluable to woodland wildlife. Even people ate the nuts in times of famine and any pigs they kept would be let loose in such woods. The great disadvantage of big beech trees is that they cast such heavy

shade little apart from a fungus or two will grow under them. So control is needed.

Lonsdale Forestry.

This company manages woodlands adjacent to Charles Wood and there is a car park for access to them. This can be found if you take the narrow minor road connecting the hamlet of Easton to Clifford Bridge. It is best approached from the Clifford Bridge end and will be found, on the right, after a short drive of a mile or less. There are three permissive walks of varying length here, with guide posts. A leaflet should normally be available at the car park.

The Lonsdale woods have only about twenty per cent of broadleaf trees; that is, those such as oak and other deciduous species, the rest being conifers like larch and Douglas fir. There are some Norway spruce (our Christmas tree) and Sitka spruce. All these are good timber trees which grow well on the damp and rather thin poor soils typical of the area: erosion over the years has washed away so much soil. Originally oak was predominant and charcoal was burnt here for use in the iron industry; in fact, you may still come across the charcoal 'hearths' dotted around these woods.

Conifers tend to be of great value to wildlife when they are only a few feet tall because they are then still so light – which encourages weeds, their seeds and therefore birds and small mammals attracted to them because of the food on offer. But when the conifers are fully grown there is far less birdlife. Darkness reigns. Hawks which may live there are not famous for their songs so silence tends to reign too: it is often a somewhat eerie silence apart maybe from a wood-pigeon flapping, say. But a very few of our smaller birds find them a suitable place to nest in: the coal tit may nest almost at ground level on the edge of a coniferous plantation and the lovely goldcrest will always choose a conifer even if it is the only one in a deciduous wood; it likes to nest high up and way out on a branch, presumably for safety reasons. The thin squeaks of both these birds can be heard here.

You will not find much in the way of ornamental conifers such as the stately cedars, though you may spot one or two specimens of the tree known as Cryptomeria japonica. You could hardly fail to spot it here because there is nothing cryptic or hidden about this tree, which will grow higher than any oak or beech if given enough shelter and moisture – and the Teign has both. Its bark is spongy and fibrous so insects like to explore and this in turn attracts insect-eating birds. The tree turns a bronze colour in winter, another fact in its favour. Larches too have much appeal for their bright green needles in spring and in autumn again for their yellow-orange tones against a background of the sombre Norway and Sitka spruce with their never-changing evergreen. But sometimes you will come across a lovely silver fir or two and these can lighten things up a bit. The wood ants play a useful part amongst these conifers. Several aphids like to feed on coniferous tree needles by sucking their sap, which can damage growth if infestations are extensive. But wood ants love aphids for the sugary honeydew they produce and will climb far up the trees in search of this.

Mammals in these woods include both roe and fallow deer, as well as dormice, now an endangered species which needs protection. Nationally this is an animal which has disappeared from huge areas of the United Kingdom where it was formerly abundant, but it hangs on in Devon, especially in old woodland edges along some of the rivers such as Bovey and Teign.

Where the paths become more open along these walks you may see a pretty plant in dry spots which has yellow flowers. It is a close relative of the foxglove and its flower is similar in shape. It is called common cow-wheat but is by no means common everywhere as it grows only on acid soil in lightly-shaded places. Where it is happy it has a long flowering period and likes grassy, heathery spots and here it may be parasitic on the roots of both grass and heather.

Castle Drogo.
Other circular walks centred on Drogo are arranged by the National Trust, for which an excellent booklet is available entitled *Walks around Castle Drogo and the Teign Valley*. The garden and woodland walks are open all the year, cost nothing and are very rewarding even if you miss all the rhododendrons and magnolias in bloom. There is also a centuries-old deer park, walled and a haven of peace. It is normally closed to the public but there is so much else of interest at Castle Drogo.

Sunny days here bring out the butterflies – at least twenty species. Like the green hairstreak, our only butterfly which is bright green underneath and when resting with wings closed looks just like a leaf, so is easily missed. Which means its enemies would miss it too: camouflage is a great survival technique. There are commoner ones like the lovely red admiral – and the peacock which seems to advertise its presence deliberately – perhaps to frighten off predator birds with those startling eyespots and the rustling noise it can make. Then there is the holly blue – often found along woodland edges if there is holly and ivy present. The holly blue lays eggs twice a year – just to make sure. Only about half a dozen of our butterflies survive the winter as adults. The first grubs hatching in the spring feed on gorse, bramble or holly, but the later batch needs the flower buds of ivy, which happens to flower long after other flowers have gone. Perhaps it is evolution rather than coincidence which makes them appear roughly at the same time. Butterfly caterpillars eat voraciously as if they know in advance that when it is their turn to perform the miracle of changing from pupa to fully-fledged adult they will not be able to eat at all. The butterflies you see on flowers or mud can only suck liquids through a tube called a proboscis as they have no proper mouth or jaws. As for adult mayflies they cannot feed or drink at all.

So the beautiful holly blue dies before winter – but what about the legendary large blue? This was a butterfly never seen at Castle Drogo but it did once exist on Dartmoor and a few selected spots elsewhere. It became extinct in the 1970s but was brought in again from abroad and introduced into five highly secret locations. Perhaps it was the extraordinary life-cycle of this butterfly which made us take the time and trouble to do so. It is completely dependent for survival on a species of ant – and the thyme plant. The disappearance of nearly all the rabbits in 1954 because of myxomatosis meant that the thyme, unable to grow tall enough, also disappeared under the tall rough grasses which sprang up and smothered it. The loss of thyme spelt disaster for the ants which depended on nectar as much as bees do, so they too died. The death of the ants was the last straw for the large blue because it relies utterly for its survival on its caterpillars being seized by the ants, which then carried them off to their nests underground. Here the ants keep the caterpillars alive by feeding them – on their own ant grubs. But this apparent generosity is strictly on the no-such-thing-as-a-free-lunch principle because the ants as a reward get necessary sugar secretions from the large blue larvae throughout the winter. In fact it stays in the dark of the ants' nest from August until the following June, by which time it has changed from caterpillar to pupa. The perfect insect then emerges from its pupa-case and slowly crawls out of the nest to lay its eggs on the buds of wild thyme and thus repeat the cycle. It is a wonderful example of the complicated interrelationships and interdependency of organisms in nature – but it is only one instance among millions of symbiosis. Inevitably, it became extinct when its habitat was no longer there to protect it.

ACKNOWLEDGEMENTS

The National Trust: I am grateful to several staff members for their help and advice – especially Adrian Shaw and Robert Taylor, Wardens of Lydford Gorge and Hembury Woods.

The Dartmoor National Park Authority: they have been patient and obliging, in particular Tess Walker, who in her former capacity as Librarian kindly placed numerous documents – and coffee – at my disposal.

The Devon Wildlife Trust: for their very useful natural history notes on woods included here.

My partner Maggie for her proof-reading and for her company on the walks.

BIBLIOGRAPHY

High Dartmoor. The standard text. Eric Hemery, 1982.

The Nature of Dartmoor. An indispensable biodiversity profile by English Nature and the DNPA.

Butterflies. Useful pocket-sized guide which includes host plants. Paul Whalley, 1979.

Insects. Another neat, portable book with extremely clear illustrations. It includes spiders. George C. McGavin, 2000.

Butterflies and Moths in Britain and Europe. David Carter, 1982.

The Dragonflies of Europe. R.R. Askew, 1988.

Where to Watch Birds in Devon & Corwall. Includes Dartmoor. D. Norman and V. Tucker, 1997.

Plant Life. C.T. Prime, 1977.

The Wild Flowers of Britain and Northern Europe. Richard Fitter and Alastair Fitter, 1974.

The Complete Guide to British Wildlife. Richard Fitter and Alastair Fitter, 1981.

Woodlands. A fascinating view of the patterns of woodland life. William Condry, 1974.

The Illustrated Book of Flowerless Plants. Frank Brightman, 1979 (Revised edition).

Mushrooms and the Fungi of Great Britain. Roger Phillips, 1981.